HELPING PEOPLE WITH DISABILITIES AND SPECIAL NEEDS THROUGH SERVICE LEARNING

AMIE JANE LEAVITT

ROSEN
PUBLISHING®

New York

Published in 2015 by The Rosen Publishing Group, Inc.
29 East 21st Street, New York, NY 10010

Copyright © 2015 by The Rosen Publishing Group, Inc.

First Edition

Library of Congress Cataloging-in-Publication Data

Leavitt, Amie Jane.
Helping people with disabilities and special needs through service
learning/Amie Jane Leavitt.—First Edition.
    pages cm.—(Service learning for teens)
Includes bibliographical references and index.
ISBN 978-1-4777-7965-1 (library bound)
1. People with disabilities—Services for—Juvenile literature. 2. Service
learning—Juvenile literature. I. Title.
HV1568.2.L43 2015
362.4'045307155—dc23

                                                          2014011465

Manufactured in the United States of America

CONTENTS

INTRODUCTION

These volunteers, including fifteen-year-old Josh *(left)*, work to fix a handicap ramp at a home that was destroyed in a tornado in Indiana.

It was a spring day in Wyoming, Michigan. The sun was shining. The birds were chirping. Yet it was no ordinary day. One suburban home housed a beehive of activity. A group of teenagers led by their teacher and a licensed contractor were busy building. Some unloaded lumber. Some were measuring and taking notes. Others were hammering, reviewing blueprints, and relaying measurements to the contractor, who was operating the power saw. Away from the building area, a few were giving the walls a fresh coat of paint. There was even a team working on the landscaping by seeding bare patches of lawn and cleaning up fallen tree limbs.

In an online video documentary about the project, Nicole Steinman, the teacher who organized the project, details what it was all about: "The students today are working on building a wheelchair ramp and fixing up a community home. The wheelchair ramp tied into our eighth grade math curriculum with the Pythagorean theorem and measuring surface area and determining certain cost needs for lumber." First, students used their math skills to design an actual ramp. Then, a licensed contractor met with the class and helped to refine their design ideas. The class also met with a disability advocate. At this meeting, students had a chance to use a wheelchair. It helped them see the challenges firsthand. After months of preparation, the students finally put all of that knowledge into action.

From the outside, the project appears to be a tremendous success. The brand new 54-foot (16.5-meter) wooden ramp will allow a wheelchair-bound person to get in and out of the home easily. The house's foundation has a nice shiny coat of white paint on it. Also, the yard has been cleared of debris, and seeds have been planted for a future lush, green lawn. But the success of the project is not just in the building.

In the video about the project, one student explains, "We're helping the people who live in this house because there's a lady and she can't get out of the house, so we're making ramps and painting the house and planting grass to make it easier for her to get out. We heard a speech and she told us how life is when you can't walk: it's hard to navigate in a wheelchair and it's hard to get into places because a lot of places don't have ramps. Now, we can see what's wrong with the community and we can know how we can help out." Another student adds, "It's really nice to help out around the community, to help people get to places that they might not be able to because of certain things they can't do."

It's not every day that you see a group of teenagers engaged in a large project like this, especially in an effort to help out a perfect stranger. So, what would possibly make this group all come together to spend their time doing such hard physical labor?

The answer is simple: service learning.

What exactly is service learning? This resource has everything you need to find out what it is and how you can take part.

CHAPTER ONE

WHAT IS SERVICE LEARNING?

Service learning is essentially the marriage between community service and academic learning. Some people think that any type of community service performed by students is service learning. That is not the case. While it's true that volunteer work is definitely a key component of service learning, there is much more involved in service learning than just the actual "service" itself. According to the National Service-Learning Clearinghouse, service learning is defined as "a teaching and learning strategy that integrates meaningful community service with instruction and reflection to enrich the learning experience, teach civic responsibility, and strengthen communities."

HIGHLY STRUCTURED ACTIVITIES

Service learning projects are highly structured, credit-bearing service activities based on the school

Service learning projects that involve working with peers can be very rewarding for students.

curriculum. Their purpose is to fulfill a real need in the community. Service learning can be applied to any subject area taught in school. The service performed by students does not stand alone. Projects also include advance preparation, post-service reflection, and some sort of demonstration or celebration of the achievement. Reflection is a key part of service learning. Without it, the students will not fully understand the real impact that the project has made on their lives and on the community. Service learning projects provide opportunities for students, faculty, and community partners to come together to achieve a common goal.

Everyone involved in service learning benefits. This was definitely true for the wheelchair-ramp project. The students benefited by learning how math concepts can be applied to the real world. They also gained an overall great feeling by doing something kind for someone in their community. The teachers were able to make a connection between schoolwork and real life for their students. Plus, they helped make the community a warmer, kinder place. The licensed contractor benefited by being able to give back to the community where he lives. He was also able to share some of his professional skills with young people. The family in the community benefited by having their home updated for their special-needs requirements. True service learning experiences are a winning situation for everyone involved.

DEEP ROOTS

The term "service learning" was coined by Robert Sigmon and William Ramsey, two educators from Atlanta, Georgia. However, combining service with education was not a new idea at the time. Many of the early educational institutions in America were founded on this ideal. Harvard College (now called Harvard University), the oldest institution of higher education in the United States, was founded in 1636. It was established to prepare its students to become actively involved citizens. The public school system in America

Service learning does not have to venture far from school. These students are bagging litter on their school grounds.

was founded on the ideals of character education, specifically that youth should be educated to be good citizens in their communities. In 1749, Benjamin Franklin discussed his ideas on this topic. He wrote a pamphlet titled *Proposals Relating to the Education of Youth in Pensilvania*. In it, he declared that "the great aim and end of all learning" was to have a desire and ability to "serve mankind, one's country, friends, and family."

This idea of combining service with learning continued with other notable educational enterprises. The Morrill Act of 1862 was signed by President Abraham Lincoln. It helped to establish land-grant colleges. With this act, each state was given a specific number of acres of federal land. The money from the sale or lease of the land was to be used to establish a major public university. The schools were mainly to educate students in practical arts like agriculture and mechanics. However, the schools and students were to provide help and support for the practical needs of the community. Many state universities today were started as land-grant colleges. In 1914, the Smith-Lever Act also encouraged students in land-grant colleges to do hands-on projects that benefited their communities.

APPROACHING THE TWENTIETH CENTURY

The Hull House was founded by Jane Addams and Ellen Gates Starr in 1889. It is another example of how academic learning was combined with service in an effort to directly benefit the community. In an article published in the *Chautauquan* magazine in 1904 titled "The Humanizing Tendency of Industrial Education," Addams described her ideas:

> A glimpse of the Hull-House shops on a busy evening incites the imagination as to what the ideal public school might offer . . . if it became really a "center" for its neighborhood. We could imagine the business man teaching the immigrant his much needed English and arithmetic and receiving in return lessons in the handling of tools and material . . . The kitchen . . . could give opportunity for Italian women to teach their neighbors how to cook the delicious macaroni . . . [In return,] the learning of English would be a comparatively easy thing for an Italian woman while she was handling kitchen utensils and was in the midst of familiar experiences.

Social worker Jane Addams is pictured here with a student from the Hull House nursery school.

At about this same time, the philosopher, social reformer, and educator John Dewey was also making his mark on the history of service learning. Dewey didn't believe that students should just memorize facts and take tests. Instead, he felt that true education was relevant and applicable to the students' lives. He believed that three qualities needed to be present for an activity to be considered educational: it had to lead to personal growth, contribute to humane conditions, and engage citizens in association with each other. In his book *Experience and Education*, he stated that the best learning comes from "the organic connection between education and personal experience." He also believed in the importance of reflection in learning. If a student didn't look back on the activity and really think about it and evaluate it, then the activity did not reach its true educational value.

A NATIONAL MOVEMENT

After the term "service learning" was first used in 1966, the idea for this type of educational experience was explored by groups of educators throughout the country.

The first conference on service learning was held in 1969 in Atlanta. Attendees discussed the pros and cons of this learning method. They proposed ideas for how it could be properly implemented in public schools, colleges, and universities in the United States. This formed the foundation for all service learning programs in schools today.

Service learning grew in the 1980s and 1990s. Several states encouraged their schools to offer service learning or made it a high school graduation requirement. In 1990, the federal government also got involved in the service learning movement when President George H. W. Bush signed the National and Community Service Act. This gave federal funds to service learning programs. Three years later, President Bill Clinton signed an act that converted this into the Corporation for National and Community Service. It

President Clinton signs the National Community Service Trust Act at the White House in 1993 as National Service volunteer youth look on.

> SERVICE LEARNING BY THE NUMBERS

Service learning became a national movement in the twenty-first century. In the 2007–2008 school year, some 4.2 million elementary, middle, and secondary school students had participated in some form of service learning in 20,400 schools throughout the nation.

A survey of state educational policies found that by the end of 2011, every state had some sort of service learning initiative. Either states passed legislation for service learning or the state boards of education had official policies encouraging the schools to use service learning in their curriculums.

Studies have proven the benefit of service learning to students. One study was conducted by the Education Commission of the States (ECS) in 2009. It showed that service learning strengthens academic engagement. It also increases school attendance, connects students to their communities, reduces risky behavior (like school violence), and decreases school dropout rates.

Some more facts from the ECS's website in 2014 show that in the United States:

•Eighty-two percent of students who are involved in service learning say that their feelings about their high school experience became more positive after taking part in service learning.

•Eighty-two percent of students polled who were not involved with service learning said that if service learning classes were offered at their school, they'd be interested in taking them.

became the central organization for AmeriCorps, Senior Corps, and Learn and Serve America.

Studies clearly show the impact of service learning. However, another way to find out what service learning does is to talk to the people who have been involved in the projects. In an interview, college student Leanna Wagner reveals her thoughts on the subject: "Service learning has been a life-changing experience. It has helped me to integrate what I am learning in class into real life situations. Service learning has also helped me to better understand the factors influencing an individual's learning. It has taught me how to work with students who have disabilities such as autism, Down syndrome, ADD/ADHD, speech impediments, and dyslexia. Service learning is a safe place for students to gain support and professional working skills. All that is required of the student is to have an open mind, a good attitude, and commitment. If you have that, then your service learning experiences will shape who you are and positively affect those you are working with."

IMPACTFUL EDUCATION

Students who participate in service learning are more likely to be engaged in civic activities as adults. They are more likely to vote and become involved in their communities. Service learning can also prepare students for future careers. Students gain an opportunity to explore various jobs and enhance job-related skills. The students who built the wheelchair ramp got first-hand experience working in design and construction. They were introduced to the basic skills of this trade. Service learning also helps establish a positive school climate where students feel a genuine bond of trust between their peers and their teachers. Service learning even educates the public. Community partners who work with students on these projects often leave with a more positive perception of teens. They have greater faith in the rising generation.

In an interview, Michigan educator Lyndsey Fischer explains, "I truly believe that our students are great people. They want to help; they want to make a difference. Some of them just don't know HOW. I think that there are so many times where we doubt what our students are capable of. They are amazing and just need the opportunity. Providing our students with this type of learning will teach them how they can make a difference in their own community. If we start with the young and continue to build and inspire, it will then be a domino effect and better our society."

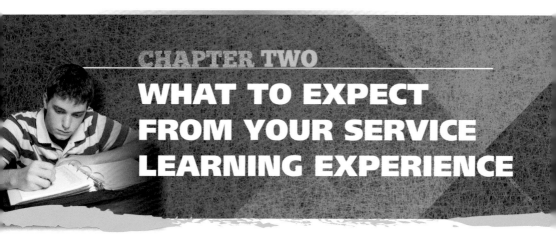

CHAPTER TWO

WHAT TO EXPECT FROM YOUR SERVICE LEARNING EXPERIENCE

O nce students have decided to get involved in service learning projects for people with special needs and disabilities, where and how should they get started? First, it's important to know the fundamentals of these projects and how they're organized.

Service learning projects are divided into four stages: preparation, action, reflection, and demonstration or celebration. In each stage, a number of activities need to be completed.

PREPARATION

In the preparation stage, the very first order of business is to identify and analyze a need. To do this, students should think about the special-needs and disabilities community in their school or town. Is there something that this group is in particular need of? For example, in a Florida high school, students found out that their town's trolley system was going to be shut down because of a lack of funding. This system was

In the preparation stage of the project, students identify a problem, then involve their teacher and people in the community to devise a solution.

the sole form of transportation for the special-needs and elderly community in their city. The students joined forces with other organizations in the community. Eventually, they helped convince city leaders to keep the system running. But they had to plan first.

Once a need has been determined and analyzed, the next step is to develop a plan. Students and teachers also have to find community partners. That's exactly what the students in Florida did for their project. It's true that they could have just tried to take on the city leaders on their own. They could have sent letters and given their opinions at city council meetings. However, one of the components of service learning is to work with community partners. By reaching out to people in community organizations, these students were able to have a larger base of support to draw upon when they approached the city leaders about this issue. This ultimately led to the success they desired.

ACTION

In service learning, the "action" is the service itself. When students are designing this stage of the project, they need to make sure that their service has a purpose and is both meaningful and effective. The activity also needs to be tied in with the school curriculum.

One school in Maryland, for example, held a disability awareness health fair. For their project, the students wanted to help their fellow students and members of the community learn about the challenges that people with disabilities face. They tied their service learning project into different curriculum areas. The project covered standards in reading, health, math, and visual arts. To plan the project, the students used their "youth voice" and took an active role. They collaborated with health care professionals. They set up and designed the fair. They also invited people to come. The students made trifold posters for their desks, PowerPoint presentations, and bookmarks that contained information about disabilities.

The youth voice component of service learning is essential to the project's success. Michigan high school teacher Lyndsey Fischer conducted a similar activity with her Teen Leadership students. They designed, planned, and held a winter carnival for the special-needs kids in their community. She is a big proponent of the importance of youth voice. "Making the service learning

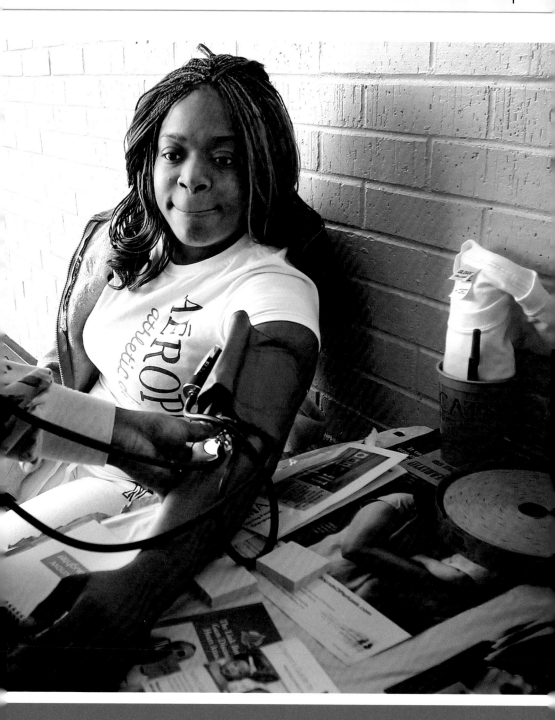

When students organize events like this health fair, they should seek support from their local medical community.

something that they are passionate about is key," she contends. "The students need to own the idea. If they come up with it, plan it, and execute it, they will have their heart in it and stay inspired."

REFLECTION

The reflection stage of service learning can come at the end of the project. It can also take place at different points throughout the project. During reflection, students describe the project. They express their thoughts and feelings about what happened in a journal or in a group discussion. They also examine the difference that the project made in their own lives and the lives of others and consider how they could improve the project for the future. During reflection, students also compare their initial ideas about the project with how they felt at the end. Most often, students who felt uneasy about service learning at the beginning end up having a very positive outlook on the experience after reflection.

Jenna Newman was a student in Baltimore County, Maryland. In 2001, she started a special charitable foundation for kids with special needs and disabilities. After working at an institute that helped children with severe disabilities, she recognized a need for funding. Many of the families she met were struggling financially because of the cost of care for their disabled children. To help with this need, Jenna designed a service learning project that she conducted on her own. In her online write-up on the Maryland Public Schools website, she summarized her process of reflection: "I kept

During reflection, service learning participants often find that they have had a very positive experience, both personally and academically.

weekly journals on my experiences and completed 24 career research projects. It is difficult not to reflect on what I see at the institute. Many of the children are severely disabled and struggle to do the simplest of tasks. It is hard to get these pictures out of mind. My experiences are always with me and I am always sharing them with my family and friends. It is hard not to be touched very deeply by what I see when I am at work."

> ## MARYLAND—DEDICATED TO SERVICE LEARNING

In 1992, Maryland became the first state in the nation to make service learning a requirement for high school graduation. "I have been in this job for 23 years which means I was here before the state mandated service learning in its graduation requirements," explains Julie Ayers, Maryland service learning specialist, in an interview. "During that time, I have seen it absolutely transform the lives of some students. Service learning is one of those strategies that cuts across life circumstances and has the potential to really engage every single type of learner."

Currently, Maryland requires its students to complete seventy-five hours of service learning in order to graduate. Students can start accumulating their hours as soon as they finish the fifth grade in some Maryland schools. Each county's school boards set their own requirements for completing service hours. This allows schools to create projects that really benefit their students and communities. After all, what might be important in an urban community might not be important in a rural one. This type of flexibility has contributed to the overall success of Maryland's service learning program, according to North Carolina State University.

Service learning has been an unfunded mandate from the beginning. Because of this lack of funding, Ayers says, "We have never had a lot of money in our state to fund specific research on the effectiveness of service learning. However, *Education Week*, a national education newspaper, did rank Maryland public schools as number one in the nation from 2008 to 2013. Obviously, this ranking cannot be directly tied to one particular part of our state's education system. Yet, service learning has been a part of Maryland public school education for 20 years, so it is part of the recipe for overall Maryland school success."

DEMONSTRATION OR CELEBRATION

In the demonstration or celebration stage of service learning, students showcase what they have learned and accomplished. They report to their peers, family, friends, or community members about their role in the project. Often during the demonstration phase, students answer key questions: *What happened in the event that was successful and meaningful? What was the importance of all of this? What should we do next?* To do this, they write articles or letters to the editor of their local newspapers. They create videos and share them online on platforms like YouTube or at school assemblies. They create websites, stage plays, or write songs about their experiences. Some design Power-Point presentations or create some kind of visual art form like a painting or mural.

The celebration is a special event. It recognizes the achievements of the project. Parents, administrators,

Eighth-grade students watch a video about diabetes, part of a yearlong disabilities awareness project. They will celebrate with an Academy Awards Night when all participants get to walk down the red carpet.

community members, and even the press can be invited to the celebration. There, students showcase the demonstrations that they have created, talk with the people who attend, snack on refreshments, and just enjoy themselves. Students may also be awarded special certificates for their achievements.

CHAPTER THREE

SERVICE LEARNING IN ACTION

Service learning is not a one-way street. It's true that students learn by being of service to others. They have an opportunity to practice academic and social skills. They even gain a wider view of the world. But service learning is not just about the students. As the stories below will show, service learning is a benefit to those being served, as well as the community at large.

PEER BUDDIES

Lime Kiln Middle School (LKMS) is located in Howard County, Maryland, directly next door to Cedar Lane School—an educational program designed specifically for students with low-incidence disabilities. Since 2005, LKMS has offered a special Peer Buddy program that allows its students to assist their peers at Cedar Lane. This program has been a tremendous success from the start. The program's instructor, Melissa Thompson, says, "That first year I thought I would be lucky to have 20 students who wanted

Service learning can also involve more physical subjects like PE. Here, high school students play a game of basketball.

to be part of the program. Yet, I had more than 128 students who wanted to participate and each year it continued to grow."

Each year since 2005, students from LKMS buddy up with students from Cedar Lane. During the school day, when students from LKMS visit Cedar Lane, they help their buddies with specific tasks. LKMS students can be found tutoring in math, helping with arts and crafts, or assisting in physical education. The middle school students help with more than just curriculum. They do everything from helping their buddies move about the school in wheelchairs, aiding their buddies in the lunchroom, and playing games with their buddies on the playground or gym. The LKMS students work with the classroom teachers at Cedar Lane to help create activities and adapt lessons that are more suited to Cedar Lane's students.

Engaging with the students at Cedar Lane helps LKMS students apply learning from all subject areas. They are able to reinforce what they learn by teaching it to their buddies. The project also requires that the LKMS students create some kind of artifact to demonstrate what they learn in the program. These artifacts can be a written report, a video, a Power-Point presentation, or some kind of creative adaptive device that would aid the Cedar Lane students with their learning. This is the "demonstration" that was discussed earlier. "I was constantly amazed every year at what the students would come up with," Thompson asserts. "Students made book holders, adaptive scissors, and pencil holders. One group of boys were concerned that their buddy couldn't roll a dice to play a board game. So, they invented a battery powered spinner that their buddy could operate using a switch. Another group made a paintbrush holder for their buddy out of plastic piping. Another Cedar Lane student had difficulty doing art projects because he lacked fine motor skills. So, his buddies

> ## STUDENT PERSPECTIVE: INTERVIEW WITH BRIGID DASS

What was your experience with the Peer Buddy program at Lime Kiln Middle School?

I originally decided to participate in Peer Buddies because I have always liked the idea of helping others and was very excited when the opportunity of working with students at Cedar Lane was presented to me. I wouldn't say I was nervous or afraid when I first started but I definitely was not sure what to expect and was anxious and excited to see what it would be like working with students with disabilities. Working with the "buddies" was such a rewarding experience and helped me learn that just because the students may have a disability they really aren't that different from you or me. I think that is super important for students to realize especially at the middle school age. My favorite part of participating in the Peer Buddies program was being able to go on field trips with the classes I worked with. Some trips we went on included going to craft stores and going out to lunch. This allowed me to help students in a social setting while getting to know them better. At the end of each year, I was required to complete a project that reflected upon my Peer Buddies experience. Although I do not exactly remember what I did for these projects, the reflecting aspect was beneficial and helped me realize how much I grew and learned.

How do you feel that the Peer Buddy program helped the kids at both Lime Kiln and Cedar Lane?

This program provides the students at Lime Kiln an opportunity to see that students that have disabilities are more similar to them than they think. Peer Buddies helps give the students at Lime Kiln a more open mind-set when working with others that may be seen as different. At the same time, Peer Buddies helps the students at Cedar Lane feel more accepted because they get to know the students at Lime Kiln. This program also helps the students at Cedar Lane with their social skills when they have the opportunity to interact with the students from Lime Kiln.

How did this particular service learning experience affect your life?

Not only did I feel like I became a better person through Peer Buddies, but it also helped me realize what I want to do with my life. I am currently a special education major at James Madison University and hope to eventually teach special education. I think the fact that Peer Buddies was such a positive experience helped my interest in serving those with special needs grow.

from LKMS made him an adaptive marker holder by drilling a hole in a tennis ball and sliding the marker inside. The student could then hold on to the tennis ball instead of the marker itself."

By the end of the project, the LKMS students gain skills in leadership, communication, academia, and problem solving. They are also more empathetic to their peers and become friends with Cedar Lane's students. Two particular incidents of friendship were especially memorable for Thompson: "During the second year, there was a group of girls who made arrangements after school hours to get together with one of the girls from Cedar Lane to just hang out and have a play date. Then, there was also a group of boys who every day would walk over to Cedar Lane and bring their buddy back to LKMS so they could all talk and eat lunch together. These were boys who really weren't all that interested in school, but they never missed a day picking up their buddy and taking him to lunch. This project clearly made an impact on all of these students' lives."

CONNECTING WITH VETS

While Peer Buddies connected students to other students, the Voice Experiences Through Service (VETS) project connects students to adults. In this case, students with disabilities participate in a project with disabled military veterans. The project started in 2007 with schools in Indiana, Maryland, and Vermont. As part of the project, students complete the service on their own, in teams of other students with disabilities, or with a partner from the general education (non-disabled) population of the school. The job of the student in this project is to work one-on-one with a veteran, find out his or her story, and then compile this story in an audio or video format for the Library of Congress's Veterans History Project.

These interviewing experiences give the students an opportunity to interact with an adult with a disability and, by doing so, see the many possibilities available to a person regardless of a special-needs situation, disability, or other type of challenge. Cate Hart Hyatt, the project coordinator in Indiana, describes how the

The Library of Congress >> American Folklife Center

SEARCH VETERANS
HISTORY PROJECT PAGES ▶ [   ] GO

VETERANS HISTORY PROJECT

ABOUT THE PROJECT

■ HOME ■ ABOUT ■ PARTICIPATE ■ DATABASE SEARCH ■ EXPERIENCING WAR ■ PARTNERS ■ STUDENTS ■ FAQs ■ NEWS

The Veterans History Project of the American Folklife Center collects, preserves, and makes accessible the personal accounts of American war veterans so that future generations may hear directly from veterans and better understand the realities of war.

▶ Frequently Asked Questions
▶ Download a Brochure (PDF)
▶ Researching the Collections
▶ Ask a Librarian
▶ Community Events and Tips
▶ Volunteer Spotlight
▶ Other Oral History Sites
▶ Contact Us

Stories can be told through...

Personal Narratives
*audio and video-taped
interviews, written memoirs*

Correspondence
*letters, postcards, v-mail
personal diaries*

Visual materials
*photographs, drawings,
scrapbooks*

**The Project collects first-hand accounts of
U.S. Veterans from the following wars:**

• World War I (1914-1920)
• World War II (1939-1946)

This screenshot from the Veterans History Project shows all the resources available to veterans to tell their story and to readers who want to learn about their experiences.

project was beneficial for all involved: "All of the students and veterans were positively touched by the information they shared through the interactions and the learning activities. Some of them have actually stayed in touch since finishing their histories. At times, students interviewed family members or friends and because of the experience, they grew close and had deeper appreciations for each other."

Beyond closer connections with family members, some students create lasting bonds with their interviewees as they share the stories of their lives. During an interview session, one veteran mentioned that he had never had the chance to get his high school diploma. He had attended the same high school as his student interviewer, but because he and his buddies had enlisted to serve in World War II, he never had the chance to graduate. The student was saddened that her veteran friend had missed out on this important commemoration. She decided to do something about it. She shared the veteran's story with her teacher. This teacher worked with the district's superintendent to arrange for a special ceremony for the veteran. Hyatt says, "The superintendent pulled all the strings she could: the band played, the gymnasium was transformed with banners, etc. It seemed that the whole town showed up to watch this man graduate. There was not a dry eye in the ceremony."

In a similar story, one veteran got choked up when he came to the school for his interview and saw the gymnasium decorated for prom, which he never got to go to as a teenager. After the student talked to her teacher, the school decided to hold a special Veterans

Prom. All of the veterans who had been interviewed by students in the school were invited to attend with their dates. "It became a community-wide celebration," Hyatt said. The interviews were not only important to the veterans and the students, but also a great benefit to the community they all lived in. This project is still impacting the lives of those who participate in it today.

BEST PROM EVER

The students at Michigan's Sparta High School know that getting out to have fun is important. They also know it can sometimes be near impossible for people with a disability. These students have mild cognitive impairments. They know firsthand that many teens and adults with disabilities don't often have a chance to socialize. Like everyone else, they want to hang out with their friends, listen to music, go out to dinner, or enjoy fun weekend activities. They also know that staying home all the time is hard on caregivers as well.

In 2006, the students in Renné Wyman's special-needs class used the methods of service learning to make a difference in the lives of their community members. They decided to host a special dinner and dance that they called Best Prom Ever. The students were involved in every stage of the planning. They chose the theme, the menu, and the music. They called around to get donations from local community partners and set a budget. They ordered balloons, purchased decorations with the class debit card, made reservations, sold tickets, helped prepare the food, and set up and took down tables on the day of the event. The first year, sixteen people came to the event. The students who planned it were very pleased with their success. Everyone had a good time. Because the first prom did so well, the school decided to make it an annual tradition.

Each year, the event became more and more popular. By 2014, 421 guests attended, and 234 people from the community came to volunteer. As the Best Prom Ever grew in size, so did the support from the community. At the 2014 event, guests were treated to many free services: salon services (hair, makeup, manicures), formal wear (dresses and suits) and accessories, limo rides, formal photos, and gift bags. "Keeping this dance free to attendees is critical and we receive many grateful and often tearful thanks for creating an event with so much BLING for free," Wyman says.

The students who planned the event were able to improve their life skills and their employability skills. They had been able to make plans, communicate effectively with the public, and then put their plans into action to put on a huge, and successful, event. The attendees benefited by having a delightful and memorable evening with their peers. People in the community benefited by knowing that they contributed to a worthwhile cause. As Wyman puts it, "I have yet to see someone witness with their own eyes even briefly the event and choose not to participate with the next dance."

The Best Prom Ever service learning project has now expanded to include more than just one big dinner dance per year. The students also put together a Halloween dinner dance in the fall. The Sparta High

School students who have participated in these programs have presented at many conferences, sharing their experiences with a variety of audiences. In fact, just days after the Best Prom Ever in 2014, the students were asked to discuss their service learning projects at the Michigan Council for Exceptional Children's annual conference in Grand Rapids. Wyman excitedly describes the outcome of this presentation. "Since many of my students get to repeat these service learning projects with two dances a year, they become experts and they KNOW what they are talking about when they present these projects publicly," she says. "Because of that, the students rocked the presentation! They gave their very first PowerPoint presentation and we even had a videographer there to capture the moment."

DISABILITY AWARENESS

The students at Holmdel High School in New Jersey get involved with the special-needs community in their own school. The school's Best Buddies program gives students in the general education population a chance to provide one-on-one service for their peers who have special needs in the school. For this program, students sign up in the fall and work with their buddies throughout the school year. Then, for the program's culminating activity in the spring, the students host a Disabilities Awareness Fair for the entire student body.

For the fair in 2013, students set up specific exhibits that highlighted various disabilities. These were meant to educate people on the challenges that

High school students Andi and Lindsy are president and director of their school's Best Buddies program.

people with special needs face. One student set up an exhibit on dyslexia. He made a poster illustrating what challenges dyslexia can cause for people. He then provided materials for students to be able to see for themselves what a person with dyslexia encounters when he or she tries to read a piece of text. At another exhibit, a student with epilepsy brought his golden retriever named Potter. During this presentation, the student explained to his peers how service animals like Potter are able to help people with specific special needs.

Students at other exhibits provided firsthand experiences of how difficult it is for a person with hearing and vision loss to perform school tasks like reading, taking tests, and listening to lectures in class. They had tunnel-vision goggles, glasses that mimicked the effects of macular degeneration, and sound-muffling equipment for participants to try out. At other exhibits, students provided hands-on experiences for their peers to show how people with physical difficulties can struggle with basic everyday activities, like buttoning a shirt.

In a video interview for the *Asbury Park Press*, student Jack Baisely, who had been involved with the program since his freshman year, proclaims, "You see these kids in the hallways all the time and you never really interact with them. [In this program,] you get to become their best friends and learn something really cool about all of them. I just think this is a really awesome program and it really helps enlighten people."

CHAPTER FOUR

THE FACES OF SERVICE LEARNING

G etting involved in service learning is a life-changing decision. In these types of projects, students make connections between themselves and their academic learning and between themselves and others. These same kinds of connections can't be made in traditional book-and-test-style learning experiences. Because of the uniqueness of service learning's hands-on instruction in the community, many students consider these projects to be the highlights of their educational experience. If the real goal of education is to frame the whole child—to educate not only his mind, but also his heart—then service learning is an effective vehicle to achieve that objective.

To really understand the impact of service learning projects, it's best to listen to the stories of the people who have actually been involved in them. Here are the stories of four people.

BETSY OTTINGER

Betsy Ottinger received her undergraduate degree in social work from Geneva College in Pennsylvania.

"Service learning was a requirement for several of my classes in college," she said. "However, my positive experiences while fulfilling these requirements led me to become involved in other elective service learning opportunities, too. These projects ranged from one-day events serving the local community with yard work, trash pickup, and painting, to 30-hour semester class requirements at community after-school programs."

People who get involved in service learning often keep on doing volunteer activities that help their communities or the world at large.

Ottinger said that the projects gently nudged her out of her comfort zone. They had a great impact: "By being around people and in environments that I may have not found myself in otherwise, I was able to learn a lot not only about concepts I was learning in the classroom, but about others and myself." One of those "gentle nudges" happened during a project with the special-needs and disabilities community. "For one of my human services classes, we went to a drop-in center for adults with mental health issues. This was definitely an intimidating, and at times uncomfortable, experience, as I previously had not had much contact with this population. By the end of the visit, my class-mates and I were much more relaxed and even had fun interacting with the clients at the center! By step-ping out of our comfort zone and confronting our insecurities, we were able to have a positive experi-ence and gain self-confidence."

KAYLA GUETTICH

Kayla Guettich participated in service learning while in high school. She said, "I was always drawn to the idea of helping others." While most projects are local, hers was global. She went all the way to Uganda, a nation in East Africa. There, she spent time helping out at a school, an orphanage, a women's empower-ment workplace, and a farm. "As I worked on projects that were making a difference in someone else's life, I found an incredible feeling of fulfillment. During this experience, I put myself in several situations that were uncomfortable and challenging. Yet, I pushed

Children in Ndende, Gabon, play a game of football with American Peace Corps volunteers.

through those feelings and as a result found utter happiness because of the friendships that I was making through the service work."

One of Guettich's favorite experiences was working with the children. "I loved working with the elementary and middle school students there. The kids loved learning and I loved to see the excitement when I taught them about the world outside of Uganda."

DIVING INTO SERVICE LEARNING

Feeling apprehensive about participating in service projects is normal. Here is advice from students and educators to help you conquer your fears.

•Kayla Guettich, student: "If you have a desire to do service learning, go out and make it happen. I promise it will be the most rewarding thing you will do in your life. Service learning gives you hands-on experience and helps to open your eyes to the real world."

•Delaney Lambert, student: "Take steps slowly and give it time. It's difficult to be a success instantaneously, so do not get discouraged if plans don't work out and seeds don't take root immediately. Be patient and repetitive, and always be on the lookout to learn something new."

•Betsy Ottinger, student: "Just do it! The educational and personal benefits of participating in service learning are well worth the fear and vulnerability of stepping out of your comfort zone. You will walk away with new experiences and a new perspective."

•Renné Wyman, educator: "Get involved. Ask yourself, what do you WANT to do? These projects can go in any direction YOU want them to go. Grab a hold and drive them."

•Jon Westover, educator: "About 95 percent of my students start out apprehensive but finish just loving the experience and learning so much and making a measurable difference in the community. So, I would say, just dive on in and give it a try. It can be a little scary at first, but faculty do a great job of providing the scaffolding and support to help students succeed. If students want to be involved in a transformative learning experience, they need to just try it!"

•Lyndsey Fischer, educator: "If students feel apprehensive, I would definitely say to them that they should really challenge themselves and step outside of their comfort zone! It is always easier to do it with others, so maybe they could invite their friends to do the same thing. They will never regret the opportunity to not only learn something themselves, but more importantly, help others who are in need. I am sure that if they try it once, it won't be their last time!"

Guettich's experience sparked a desire to join the Peace Corps after high school. "I am forever changed because of this experience," she revealed. "I found a source of happiness from doing this service work. I am more grateful now and proud of all that I have in life. I feel more positive and optimistic after returning from this experience."

DELANEY LAMBERT

College student Delaney Lambert initially became involved with service learning through the Azusa Reads, Writes, and Counts program at Azusa Pacific University in California. She spent her afternoons in the library helping elementary students with their language arts assignments. At first, she mainly helped students in general education, but then her supervisor asked her to help two children who had autism and Down syndrome. "At first I was apprehensive, but a tugging on my heart led me to help these two children, so I gave it a try," she said. "The first few sessions of tutoring were a little rough because I was still figuring out the specific needs and learning styles of each child. However, by sticking

College student Delaney Lambert was nervous about working with special-needs kids at first, but she quickly found out that they had a lot to offer her, too.

with it, I gradually learned and each study session got just a little bit better. I learned what captures the interest of each child, what ways to communicate, and how they learn best. Now, I am no longer nervous, but excited, and look forward to seeing them each day."

Lambert understands that other people might feel apprehensive about helping out in the special-needs and disabilities community because she felt that way,

Service learning projects often prove that people with disabilities and special needs are not so different from others.

too. However, because of her highly positive experience, she has nothing but encouraging advice. "Most people have a sense of uneasiness or apprehension around people with special needs because they function differently than the average person. However, special-needs people are not really that different than any of us. We all require interaction, friendship, love, and understanding; the only difference is that special-needs children have a dissimilar way of asking for it. With training and experience, I believe people will learn to accommodate special-needs children more thoroughly. With that, we will all grow closer together as a community by working together and appreciating everyone."

She added that the experience had a personal benefit. "I look forward to seeing both of my special-needs students every day. They make me laugh greater than some of my best friends, and they know how to share and love better than anyone I know."

MICHAEL FROM RHODE ISLAND

On the Rhode Island Development Disabilities Council website, several students are featured who had particularly impactful experiences with service learning. Michael (whose last name is excluded on the website) is one of these students. Michael has a mobility impairment that requires him to use a wheelchair. His story is particularly significant because it shows how people who are in the special-needs community themselves can benefit by participating as one of the servers in a service learning project.

Michael volunteered on the Rhode Island College campus for two months. During that time, he developed telephone and other communication skills to complete his tasks. He also worked directly with the children in elementary school classrooms. A photo on the website shows Michael reading a book to a group of young children.

"I was needed in the classroom to teach the kids that we're all different but similar at the same time," Michael wrote on the website. "I have taught them to not be afraid if they encounter another person in a wheelchair. If I didn't help the kids, they would always wonder why people are in wheelchairs. If I talk to these kids about it, they might go to their parents and tell them all the positive things they learned about people in wheelchairs. I would like to learn about kids and hope that they like me as much as I like them."

CHAPTER FIVE

REACHING OUT WITH SERVICE LEARNING

The number and type of service learning projects available is limited only by each student's creativity. So, how does a person get those creative juices flowing in order to come up with ideas for these projects?

GENERATING IDEAS

One way to brainstorm ideas is to list out the subject areas that are offered in the school curriculum and then think about how each area relates to people with special needs and disabilities. For example, think about physical education and the difficulties that people with special needs and disabilities may have in this class. How would a child in a wheelchair be able to play a class game like basketball? Would this child need special rules or special accommodations in order to play? These questions can lead to a very meaningful service learning opportunity. Students can then create some kind of strategy to help special-needs students play the game with their general education peers.

Service projects can take the form of repair work that can help people with disabilities have access to places they otherwise might not.

Students are encouraged to keep their eyes and ears open as they go about their daily lives. Perhaps while walking along a sidewalk that has no handicap access, imagine how difficult that would be for a person with a disability. A snowy parking lot is hard enough to navigate. Students might recognize that it is even more difficult for a person with special needs to navigate through the ice and sludge. Both of these are real-world problems that can be addressed with service learning. In these two specific examples, students can think about ways to improve the situation and then begin the planning and action phases of the project. Students in Michigan's Saline school district conducted a service learning project using this method. First, they learned about the difficulties that people with special needs have trying to get access to parking, buildings, and public places. Then students visited businesses with a "report card." The card they created rated businesses for accessibility. The students gave these cards along with suggestions on how each company could improve access to its building.

FINDING COMMUNITY PARTNERS AND FUNDING

Partnerships for service learning projects can be found in many different places. Business people are often willing to participate. In the wheelchair-ramp example from the introduction, mathematics students collaborated with a licensed contractor. He helped them with their initial design work and with building the ramp. For

It is important to have meetings to discuss what role each person will play in the project. Community members can enhance a service learning project by volunteering goods or services.

the Best Prom Ever project, students made dozens of calls to gain support from community members and local businesses. As a result, they had hair salons, real estate companies, and other businesses offer up their services. The prom is a free event. The service learning team had to raise all the funds, about $10,000, to make it happen. Many services and goods were donated by the community. Hundreds of people volunteered to help out before and after the event. People made more than four hundred cupcakes, donated sparkling grape juice for the evening's toast, and assisted with DJ and photography services. Besides making calls, the students also used the local media—radios and newspapers—to spread the word.

Nonprofit organizations, service clubs, government offices, community colleges, and universities are other places where students can find support and funding for their service learning projects. A local nonprofit foundation called the Grand Rapids Awesome Foundation donated a large sum of money in 2012 to help the Best Prom Ever be successful. There are other national organizations that might be able to help out with service learning–related projects. Goodwill, Boys & Girls Clubs of America, Lions Club, Habitat for Humanity, American Legion, American Red Cross, Rotary Club, Special Olympics, YMCA, Kiwanis Club, and the Salvation Army are all organizations that serve the community. These organizations may not be able to provide funding, but they might be able to offer support and partnerships that can lead to success.

Community partnerships can also come from

During reflection, remember to get everyone who participated in the project to share their experiences.

#1 IN SERVICE

From 2006 to 2013, the annual *Volunteering and Civic Life in America* research report has rated Utah the number one volunteering state in the nation. The report has found that 47.7 percent of Utah adults volunteer. That is nearly double that of the national average of 26.5 percent.

One of Utah's largest universities, Utah Valley University (UVU), just celebrated the school's twentieth anniversary of service learning. Jon Westover, the director of academic learning at UVU, stated, "As of 2014, the school has more than 6,000 students every year who take service learning designated courses. That number does not include non-designated courses that do service learning, nor does it include other volunteer/community-engagement participation."

Westover strongly believes in the importance of engaging with the community. He said, "In service learning, students gain valuable hands-on immersion into their field of study, community partners gain valuable resources in the form of the student/faculty human capital contribution to the service-learning project, and faculty have the opportunity to truly mentor and coach students toward success. For everyone involved, I feel lives are changed. Speaking specifically to students, they have an enhanced sense of civic commitment, they often become more comfortable with diversity, ambiguity, and nuance, and they develop valuable skills that will help them find success in their future lives."

When Matthew Chambers was a student at UVU, he helped the Volunteer and Service Learning Center on campus. This center works with campus departments and faculty to organize various activities focused on service learning. The projects organized by the center vary depending upon coursework and community need. For example, in a graphic design course, students can create marketing materials for a local nonprofit so the organization can better reach its community. In a project management course, students can perform an assessment for a local food bank to help improve overall customer service. In an interview, Chambers explained that through his observations of student projects, he noticed that the students who participated "were unified and forgot themselves in serving others." He also saw that the service learning projects helped students "become connected with real issues that they would normally ignore day to day. It brought people together to discuss what was being accomplished; it started the conversation." He feels that service learning is helpful because it "puts people in an uncomfortable environment that stimulates the mind and then helps people feel positive about the contributions they have made. Because of that, it increases societal happiness."

parents. Parents have their own connections through work, houses of worship, neighbors, and friends whom they can enlist for help in service learning projects. These contacts can be people who help out by donating their time and talents for the project or people who help out with funding. Parents themselves can also be partners. They might have specific skill

Service learning can impact the future careers of students by showing them different career paths and by giving them some of the skills they would need to be successful.

sets that could be helpful for the project.

GETTING A PLAN IN ORDER

Before students call a community partner, plans have to be solidified. Businesses will not get involved with or donate to a project that is disorganized. Students need a clear plan of what will happen for the entire event. They also need to know what role the community partner will be asked to play.

Once the community partner has agreed to help, the next crucial step is to communicate. Make sure the partner is kept up to date on all the happenings with the project. Let participants know about key deadlines well in advance. E-mail or phone reminders are a great way to do this.

Most community partners also like to be included in the reflection activities and celebrations. They should be given an opportunity to express their opinions on how the project went and how it could be improved. After all, they are partners. That means that their feedback has equal weight. In addition, community partners should be made to feel appreciated for their time, efforts, and funding. Heartfelt thank-you notes are a must. This will help the community partners feel more inclined to help out next time.

JUST GET STARTED

The most important part of any service learning project comes at the beginning. It should be the students' own initiative to just dive in and get going. If service learning is something you're interested in, don't wait. Get started now. Look around for needs in your community. Brainstorm ideas for projects. Make a clear plan and then get support from community partners. Put your plan into action and then reflect on your progress and celebrate your success.

Service learning can make a huge difference in the world, especially in the area of special needs and disabilities. Students who participate in these projects are able to see the world as a cohesive place where everyone is important and can make a difference. Coming up with ideas for projects in this area of service learning can be both fun and rewarding. Students may form new friendships and gain new skills. They may even find new ways of looking at the world.

It's safe to say that the majority of students who take

the time to really engage in service learning experiences for people with special needs and disabilities will be impacted for the rest of their lives. That has been the case for every person interviewed here. Many of the interviewees have gone on to pursue careers related to their service learning experiences. Some went into social work, others went into education, others have decided to join the Peace Corps, and others desire to eventually work at or start nonprofit organizations. All of the interviewees mentioned how powerful their service learning experiences were for them and how they're sure that the memories of those experiences will stay with them for a lifetime.

The words of Brooke Strong Vaquerano, a student who participated in service learning while in college, echo the feelings of the others when she declares, "I am a firm believer that if everyone participated in service learning, we would live in a much better world. We would have the world peace we are always longing for. Service learning really helps you to see the good in people. It helps you to see that you can make a difference. Even if the difference is changing yourself to be a better person, that difference alone makes the world a better place."

GLOSSARY

adaptive Adjusted so as to help a disabled person more easily perform a certain activity.

ambiguity Something that lacks a clear meaning.

assessment An evaluation, idea, or opinion about something.

autism A disorder that causes impaired social interaction and communication.

brainstorm To generate ideas in order to solve a problem in a group.

cognitive Of or relating to mental function.

collaborate To work together jointly on an activity.

component One of the parts of something.

contractor A professional who manages a construction project.

curriculum The planned educational content that students will learn.

designated Chosen for a specific purpose.

documentary A nonfiction educational film or movie.

Down syndrome A genetic disorder caused by an extra chromosome and associated with growth delays and mild to moderate intellectual disability.

dyslexia A developmental reading disorder.

enhanced Improved in quality or desirability.

enlist To join; often used to refer to joining the military.

impairment Any loss or abnormality of bodily function.

initiative The opportunity and drive to do something before being prompted or before others do it.

interviewees People who are interviewed.

macular degeneration A chronic eye disease that causes vision loss.

mandated Required or ordered.

nonprofit organization An organization that does not make money off of its work.

nuance A subtle difference or quality.

Pythagorean theorem A mathematical formula that allows a person to determine the lengths of the sides in a right triangle.

speech impediment Any communication disorder where normal speech is interrupted, such as stuttering or a lisp.

FOR MORE INFORMATION

Campus Compact National Office
45 Temple Place
Boston, MA 02111
(617) 357-1881
Website: http://www.compact.org
Campus Compact is the only national higher educa-
    tion association that promotes campus-based civic
    engagement. More than 1,100 colleges and univer-
    sities (public, private, two-year, and four-year) are
    joined together in this association.

Canadian Alliance for Community Service-Learning
2128 Dunton Tower
Carleton University
1125 Colonel By Drive
Ottawa, ON K1S 5B6
Canada
(613) 520-2600, ext. 8241
Website: http://www.communityservicelearning.ca/en
Community service learning in Canada has been evolv-
    ing over the past decade since it was pioneered by
    Nova Scotia's St. Francis Xavier University in 1999.
    This organization's vision is that students, educa-
    tors, and communities throughout Canada will learn
    and work together in an effort to improve society.

Corporation for National & Community Service
1201 New York Avenue NW
Washington, DC 20525
(202) 606-5000
Website: http://www.nationalservice.gov

This is the official website for a federal agency that helps more than five million Americans improve their lives, the lives of others, and their communities through service. The agency includes AmeriCorps, Senior Corps, the Social Innovation Fund, the Volunteer Generation Fund, and so forth.

J.W. McConnell Family Foundation
1002 Sherbrooke W., Suite 1800
Montreal, QC H3A 3L6
Canada
(514) 288-2133
Website: http://www.mcconnellfoundation.ca
This foundation provides grants to universities in Canada that are engaging in service learning projects and activities. In addition, the foundation provides a grant to the Canadian Alliance for Community Service-Learning so the ideals of service learning can be spread to a larger national audience.

National Coalition for Academic Service-Learning (NCASL)
Innovations in Civic Participation
1776 Massachusetts Avenue NW, Suite 201
Washington, DC 20009
(202) 775-0290
Website: http://www.ncasl.org
NCASL's primary purpose is to provide leadership and support for state agencies and educational professionals who are trying to institute service learning in the K–12 classroom. Through its advocacy of service learning, the organization hopes to promote

schools that have a positive climate where all students are valued and are becoming contributing members of their communities.

National Service-Learning Clearinghouse
4 Carbonero Way
Scotts Valley, CA 95066
(866) 245-7378
Web site: http://gsn.nylc.org
This resource provides a wide variety of information regarding service learning, including ideas for projects, groups to join, discussions to follow, and topics to research. There are different areas of the site specifically suited for students and educators.

WEBSITES

Because of the changing nature of Internet links, Rosen Publishing has developed an online list of websites related to the subject of this book. This site is updated regularly. Please use this link to access this list:

http://www.rosenlinks.com/SLFT/Disab

FOR FURTHER READING

Bringle, Robert G., Julie A. Hatcher, and Steven G. Jones, eds. *International Service Learning: Conceptual Frameworks and Research* (IUPUI Series on Service Learning Research). Sterling, VA: Stylus Publishing, LLC, 2011.

Butin, Dan W. *Service-Learning in Theory and Practice: The Future of Community Engagement in Higher Education.* New York, NY: Palgrave Macmillan, 2010.

Cipolle, Susan Benigni. *Service-Learning and Social Justice: Engaging Students in Social Change.* Lanham, MD: Rowman & Littlefield, Inc., 2010.

Cress, Christine M., Peter J. Collier, and Vicki L. Reitenauer, et al. *Learning Through Serving: A Student Guidebook for Service-Learning and Civic Engagement Across Academic Disciplines and Cultural Communities.* Sterling, VA: Stylus Publishing, 2013.

Dolgon, Corey, and Chris Baker. *Social Problems: A Service Learning Approach.* Thousand Oaks, CA: Pine Forge Press, 2011.

Farber, Katy. *Change the World with Service Learning: How to Create, Lead, and Assess Service Learning Projects.* Plymouth, England: Rowman & Littlefield Education, 2011.

Flecky, Kathleen, and Lynn Gitlow. *Service-Learning in Occupational Therapy Education: Philosophy & Practice.* Sudbury, MA: Jones and Bartlett Publishers, LLC, 2011.

Gent, Pamela J. *Great Ideas: Using Service Learning and Differentiated Instruction to Help Your Students Succeed.* Baltimore, MD: P. H. Brooks Publishing Company, 2009.

Goldberg, Louise. *Yoga Therapy for Children with Autism and Special Needs.* New York, NY: W. W. Norton & Company, 2013.

Jones, Ron. *The Acorn People.* New York, NY: Laurel Leaf, 1996.

Kaye, Cathryn Berger. *The Complete Guide to Service Learning: Proven, Practical Ways to Engage Students in Civic Responsibility, Academic Curriculum, & Social Action.* Minneapolis, MN: Free Spirit Publishing, Inc., 2010.

Lan Lin, Phylis, ed. *Service-Learning in Higher Education: National and International Connections.* Indianapolis, IN: University of Indianapolis Press, 2011.

Lewis, Barbara A. *The Kid's Guide to Service Projects: Over 500 Service Ideas for Young People Who Want to Make a Difference.* Minneapolis, MN: Free Spirit Publishing, Inc., 2009.

Mannix, Darlene. *Life Skills Activities for Secondary Students with Special Needs.* San Francisco, CA: John Wiley & Sons, Inc., 2009.

Mannix, Darlene. *Social Skills Activities for Secondary Students with Special Needs.* San Francisco, CA: John Wiley & Sons, Inc., 2009.

National Youth Leadership Council. *Getting Started in Service-Learning: An Elementary Through High School Handbook.* St. Paul, MN: National Youth Leadership Council, 2010.

Robinson, Jerry W., Jr., and Gary Paul Green, eds. *Introduction to Community Development: Theory, Practice, and Service-Learning.* Thousand Oaks, CA: Sage Publications, 2011.

Steinbeck, John. *Of Mice and Men.* New York, NY: Penguin, 1937.
Sundem, Garth. *Real Kids, Real Stories, Real Change: Courageous Actions Around the World.* Minneapolis, MN: Free Spirit Publishing, Inc., 2010.
Tada, Joni Eareckson. *Special Needs Smart Pages: Advice, Answers and Articles About Teaching Children with Special Needs.* Delight, AR: Gospel Light Publishing, 2009.

BIBLIOGRAPHY

Addams, Jane. "The Humanizing Tendency of Industrial Education." *Chautauquan*, Volume 39, March–August 1904, p. 266.

Asbury Park Press. "Disabilities Awareness Day, Holmdel High School." App.com. Retrieved March 17, 2014 (http://www.app.com/VideoNetwork/2325188434001/Holmdel-students-host-Disabilities-Awareness-Day).

Ayers, Julie. Interview by author, phone, February 2014.

Cauley, Kate. "Integrating Student Learning Objectives with Community Service Objectives Through Service Learning in Health Professions Schools Curricula." Community-Campus Partnerships for Health, April 29–May 2, 2000. Retrieved March 27, 2014 (https://depts.washington.edu/ccph/pdf_files/TR1.PDF).

Chambers, Matthew. Interview by author, e-mail, February 25, 2014.

CMC Education. "Community House Ramp." CMC Education YouTube Channel. Retrieved March 27, 2014 (https://www.youtube.com/watch?v=EdFFMBfnXHg).

Cortez, Marjorie. "Utah Tops Nation for Volunteerism 8 Years Running." Deseret News, December 16, 2013. Retrieved March 17, 2014 (http://www.deseretnews.com/article/865592525/Utah-tops-nation-for-voluntarism-8-years-running.html?pg=all).

Cunningham, Jeffrey. "Sparta Seeks Funding to Make 'Best Prom Ever' Even Better." MLive.com, September 7, 2012. Retrieved March 27, 2014 (http://www.mlive.com/sparta/index.ssf/2012/09/sparta_seeks_funding_to_make_b.html).

Dass, Brigid. Interview by author, e-mail, March 15, 2014.

Dewey, John. *Experience and Education.* Indianapolis,
    IN: Kappa Delta Pi, 1938. Retrieved March 17, 2014
    (http://www.schoolofeducators.com/wp-content/
    uploads/2011/12/EXPERIENCE-EDUCATION-JOHN
    -DEWEY.pdf).
Fischer, Lyndsey. Interview by author, e-mail, March
    14, 2014.
Franklin, Benjamin. *Proposals Relating to the Education of
    Youth in Pensilvania.* Philadelphia, 1749. Penn
    University Archives & Records Center. Retrieved
    March 17, 2014 (http://www.archives.upenn.edu/
    primdocs/1749proposals.html).
Guettich, Kayla. Interview by author, e-mail, March
    5, 2014.
"History of Service-Learning in Higher Education."
    National Service-Learning Clearinghouse, January
    2008. Retrieved March 27, 2014 (http://www.fsu
    .edu/~flserve/resources/resource%20files/History_
    of_SL_in_HE_FINAL_May08.pdf).
Hyatt, Cate Hart. Interview by author, e-mail, February
    25, 2014.
Institute for Emerging Issues. "Promote Service Learn-
    ing." North Carolina State University. Retrieved March
    27, 2014 (http://iei.ncsu.edu/emerging-issues/
    ongoing-programs/generation-z/taking-action/
    promote-service-learning).
Kenny, Maureen, Lou Ann K. Simon, Karen Kiley-Brabeck,
    and Richard M. Lerner, eds. *Learning to Serve:
    Promoting Civil Society Through Service Learning.*
    Norwell, MA: Kluwer Academic Publishers, 2002.
Lambert, Delaney. Interview by author, e-mail, February
    27, 2014.

Newman, Jenna. "Jenna Fund for Kids in Need." Maryland Public Schools. Retrieved March 17, 2014 (http://www.marylandpublicschools.org/NR/rdonlyres/69F1D6B6-C70D-4451-96F5-FF4FAA6D699A/25298/TheJennaFundforKidsinNeed.pdf).

Ottinger, Betsy. Interview by author, e-mail, February 24, 2014.

Steinman, Nicole, and Tammy Annis. "Wheelchair Ramp." KentISD.org. Retrieved March 14, 2014 (http://www.kentisd.org/instructional-services/health-safety-service-learning/service-learning/projects/middle-school-projects/wheelchair-ramp).

Taylor, James E. *An Assessment of the Practices and Strategies that Contribute to the Success of High School Service-Learning Programs.* Digital Commons at Georgia Southern University, Fall 2010. Retrieved March 27, 2014 (http://digitalcommons.georgiasouthern.edu/cgi/viewcontent.cgi?article=1372&context=etd).

Thompson, Melissa. Interview by author, phone, March 10, 2014.

Vaquerano, Brooke Strong. Interview by author, e-mail, February 22, 2014.

Wagner, Leanna. Interview by author, e-mail, March 14, 2014.

Westover, Jon. Interview by author, e-mail, February 20, 2014.

Wyman, Renné. Interview by author, e-mail, March 12, 2014.

INDEX

ABOUT THE AUTHOR

Amie Jane Leavitt, a graduate of Brigham Young University, is an accomplished author and researcher who has written more than sixty books for young people. She has also worked as a consultant, writer, and editor for numerous educational publishing and assessment companies. To check out a listing of Ms. Leavitt's current projects and published works, check out her website at www.amiejaneleavitt.com.

PHOTO CREDITS

Cover Jaren Jai Wicklund/Shutterstock.com; p. 3 bymandesigns/Shutterstock.com; pp. 4–5, 22–23, 28 © AP Images; p. 8 FuzzBones/Shutterstock.com; p. 9 Jacom Stephens/Vetta/Getty Images; p. 11 Hill Street Studios/Sarah Golonka/Blend Images/Getty Images; p. 13 Wallace Kirkland/Time & Life Pictures/Getty Images; p. 15 Cynthia Johnson/Time & Life Pictures/Getty Images; p. 19 © iStockphoto .com/eurobanks; p. 20 Buero Monaco/Taxi/Getty Images; p. 25 Simone Becchetti/E+/Getty Images; p. 29 Flashon Studio/Shutterstock .com; p. 30 Rayman/Photodisc/Getty Images; p. 40 © Laura Embry/U-T San Diego/ZUMA Press; p. 42 Antonio Guillem/Shutterstock.com; p. 43 Ron Levine/Digital Vision/Getty Images; p. 45 James P. Blair/National Geographic Image Collection/Getty Images; pp. 48–49 Richard Hutchings/Photo Researchers/Getty Images; p. 50 Simone Becchetti/Vetta/Getty Images; p. 53 Tom Wang/Shutterstock.com; p. 54 Bloomberg/Getty Images; pp. 56–57 Creatas Images/Thinkstock; pp. 58–59 svetikd/E+/Getty Images; pp. 62–63 Goodluz/Shutterstock.com; cover and interior pages background textures and patterns vector illustration/Shutterstock.com, Apostrophe/Shutterstock.com, nattanan726/Shutterstock.com, Yulia Glam/Shutterstock.com; back cover silhouette Pavel L Photo and Video/Shutterstock.com.

Designer: Michael Moy; Editor: Tracey Baptiste; Photo Researcher: Karen Huang